Nothing Gold

Robyn Kusnetsova

DEDICATION

FOR

MY

SIPAHI

Contents

ACKNOWLEDGMENTS

I wish to extend my heartfelt thanks, first and foremost to my parents, Brian and Daphne Smith, for giving me life, and doing their best to guide me through its treacherous waters.

To my children, Evelyn and Christopher Rennie, who have been my world, my greatest joy, and have loved me unconditionally.

To my dear sisters, nephews, nieces and friends, who have served as examples to me, and helped me to realise the kind of person I truly want to be.

Each and every one of you, have inspired and spurred me on in your own way, and there are no words which can convey, or express, how much that has meant.

To the following, living and gone, I owe special mention. This book would never have seen the light of day, without you.

Marcus Doles
Rajesh Kumar Varma
Nick and Alison Miller
Jack and Samantha Godkin
Robert Goulding and Dava Fuller
Henry Guiste
Eddie Cousins
Garth Taylor
Gladys Morrison
Joyce Thomas-Smith
Rohini O'Connor
Nadine Juignet
Keyan Answer
Anthony Kung
Janita-Lenee Holloway
June Munroe
Shelly Ann Panton
John Parsons
Janet Silvera
Runa Srivastava
Shanti-Harjani Williams

No One Sees...

She tries her best. She is convinced that no-one sees...

She drags her weary bones out of bed, hearing the familiar cry, piercing the lonely silence at four in the morning. He cannot help her. Only she, can suckle their child." Go back to sleep," she whispers to him. You have work, tomorrow. Your crucial meeting. Please. You need your rest. It is the third time tonight, that she has woken. She, and her little cherub, rock gently in her Grandmother's chair.

The baby has been bathed; the breakfast made; his shirt, suit and tie, lain on the bed. She wants to hold him. To shut the world out, for just a little while... but, his phone rings, and once again the baby begins to cry. A kiss on the forehead, and he flies through the front door. The engine in the driveway purrs, as she holds and sings, to their beautiful, fractious daughter. There seems to be no comforting the little one, today. She worries. She always worries. Am I a good enough mother, to her? Am I a good enough wife, to my husband? Is he feeling neglected? Am I finding enough time, for "us?" He never seems to be home any more. The Banana Bread she baked for him - his favourite - is in the oven, burning, She doesn't notice, for she is far too preoccupied; patience strained. As she screams another anxious lullaby...

The baby has barely slept, today. It was just a case of colic, the doctor had said. Her fretting has finally stopped, but not her fussing; checking on her angel every few minutes, even now that she has, at last, managed to settle. There is still much to do... changing the sheets, that next load of laundry, trying once more to bake her husband's treat, before he returns home; preparing the three-course meal. Cutting some fresh hydrangeas from the garden, to decorate the table. Calling the carpenter, to repair the broken floorboard on the landing, at the top of the stairs. No. She mustn't forget to do that. Oh, and some candles. They both love dining by candlelight. She must make a quick trip to the store, when the baby wakes.

She wants it to be special, tonight. She wants to make HIM feel special, tonight. Because she understands, that while she struggles and feels as though she can never accomplish enough, he toils, sweats, and fights his own battles; each and every day. To outwit, and outshine, his competitors. To impress, in order to access; the kind of opportunities (so often fleeting), which will see his fledgling business thrive. Yes, he is ambitious. Even relentless... yet, who is it really all for? For her. And her. She knows it, and wants him to realize how much she appreciates him. If only she could rest for ten minutes, before setting about completing all her remaining tasks...

*****

She tells him to go back to sleep. He never does, until his daughter, and wife, are safely back in bed, and dreaming whatever it is that mothers, and tiny babies, dream. His watchful eye never wavers. His fervour to protect them, never wanes. He is exhausted, but he never complains. He sees that she is exhausted, too. Even frail, sometimes. He would do anything he could, to make it easier for her. He wants to whisk her away. He wants to show her, in the passionate way that he used to, how much a part of him, she is. That his love for her is stronger than ever before; but, life keeps getting in the way. The doorbell sounds. The phone rings. He has to go. Someone invariably makes demands upon his time.

He tries to prioritize, but there are never enough hours in the day. So often, he feels like throwing in the towel, but then, it dawns on him. That he cannot, must not, abdicate from his responsibility, and higher purpose. It is all for them. These cherished blossoms, in whom all his hopes and dreams, reside. They are depending on him. To love them; to provide for them; to keep them safe; in an increasingly unsafe, and brutal, world.

He eventually comes home. He finds his darling wife lying, curled up, on the couch in their front room. His heart threatens to burst within his chest, so much love floods through him, as he gazes down upon her. He resolves not to disturb her slumber. Heaven knows, how much she needs this rest. He gently pulls the blanket up, over her delicate shoulders. He would give his whole Kingdom, for a kiss upon her shoulder… he wonders, whether or not she knows, how proud he is of her; with everything that she goes through. For his sake, and for their

daughter's. He wishes that there was something else she could know. That he is doing everything he possibly can. He wonders whether it is enough, even as he is painfully aware, that it is all he has to give. It won't occur to her, he thinks, and tells himself that it doesn't matter. Tomorrow, the sun will rise; just as he will rise, and strive to do it all again.

He tries his best. He is convinced no one sees…

Thoughts of Freedom

Now, having reached my fourth decade of life, I have begun to take stock of all that I have overcome. All that I have moved past, to outgrow. All that I must let go, lest I become embittered, and dark of soul. It is a choice I must make, to heal. Every day. This day, and henceforth. With no codicils, and no excuses.

I have made the decision, and so it is… I must move past many things. Past relatives who gladly offer criticism and toxic "correction," real support, forthcoming. Past the fear attached to trying with all my might, to live up to their expectations (realistic, or not), of me. Past girls with their petty jealousy and feigned friendships, whispering sweet words to my face, turning them to daggers in the instant that I turn my back.

I am "over" boys whose only purpose in life is to satisfy their own desires, at my, or someone else's expense. Who, mired in shallowness, are intimidated by the sharpness of my mind, or the truth and wisdom of which I speak. I have long outgrown those who would claim to care, and yet secretly rejoice in the shadows over any misfortune which may befall me, or whenever, perchance, I truly, and catastrophically, fail.

I have learned to spot the signs, which auger darkness; and I turn my face firmly toward the light, instead. I now see through those who would happily share the spoils when times are good, yet are conveniently quick to flee, when times are hard, and burdens must be borne. I have lost respect for those who sit on the fence; with neither conscience, nor moral compass. Standing for nothing. Complacent to cruelty, and injustice. Utterly uncaring, until, or unless, misfortune touches them. As written in Edmund Burke's poignant quote, "The only thing necessary for the triumph of evil, is for good men to do nothing."

I have grown tired of the propaganda of the media and the perceived wisdom of society, telling me to always be cautious, if not overcome by fear, so that I may be kept compliant, and subjugated. \telling me, and countless others, how far they fall short. I am not intelligent enough, beautiful enough, sexy enough, wealthy enough, 'white' enough; to be considered a person of value, or worth.

I must constantly work to conquer my tendency, to fill my mind with self-doubt, and deny my better judgment and instincts, in favour of that of others. Others, in whose self-interest they are espoused, though through manipulative pretence, or a compulsion to control, are disguised as being in mine.

I have to exercise the courage and strength, to outgrow anyone, or anything, refusing to acknowledge the essence of my spirit, and actively act to block its edification, and enrichment. I have grown through, and must continue to, a great many things. Violent adversity, and covert sabotage, my teachers. Shuddering through the excruciating pain; emerging as the Queen I was born to be. Not in conceit, but in confidence. And I have never felt, or been, more free!

The Birdsong Which Lifts Us

In the darkness always looming before dawn, the news awash with nought but grim tragedy,, threat to peace, and prophesying snow, I heard the faint call of a young tawny owl. Her exclamation seemed as a charm; a shield, somehow, against despair. I could not see her (for she was, likely, too far away), but in that moment, a heron flew over the valley and gave her own, shrill, cry. It was a formed of ice and steel, yet fleeting.

Meanwhile, returning to the dominance of my eyes, I craned my neck in rotation, as my eyes followed the flight of a raven. He passed directly over my head. With this bird, there was silence... but my heart lifted as he came into view once more, with his broad, black body, and fanned-diamond tail.

Celtic, Norse and Greek mythologies, hold that ravens are the messengers of the gods. They are bold, yet playful, creatures... and among the most robust of their kind, being the first to breed, every year. The worst of winters, and bleakest of times for us, is a time of acrobatics, mating and nesting, for them. My mind drifted to the words of Percy Bysshe Shelley, as he questioned the wind... "Oh wind, if winter comes, can spring be far behind?" And the snow did not come, that day. Instead, the sky paled, hardening into a searing, steely-blue.

I continued my wanderings., and thought of my Grandfather. He longed for a life such as theirs, on outstretched wings, to soar. Majestic. I entered a wood to the sound of a proud, almost priapic, shout. A pheasant? Fodder for every predator. How paradoxically absurd, for this creature to emanate such awesome noise, given where Mother Nature has seen fit to place him. I spotted a pair, feeding; the emerging sun burnishing their plumage, so that they seemed to glow in shades of shimmering green, amber, and fiery red. A skein of geese; a tumble of gulls; the sky was filled, this day. Their white, in contrast to the brilliant blue, making this canvas more intense than it had ever seemed before.

Like all of us, these animals have less energy to expend on spurious activities, in the months of this brutal season. Yet still, their song remains. Ribald, piercing, but cherished. Times are hard. Cold as cruelty, or so to me, it often appears. All the more reason, for expressing joy. Joy, in all its conceivable forms, and drawing pleasure from life's simplest things. Keeping faith in God, the Universe, Mother Nature; however, or whoever, we perceive them to be. Cleaving to one another. Bound by the ever-turning wheel, in the ineffable knowledge that fairer, warmer days, shall surely come again.

Peaceful Now

(Behind My Heart)

The poem trapped behind my heart,

Which no one living knows,

The barren ground within my soul,

Where nothing ever grows…

This scarr-ed womb and broken back,

From torture and loaned pain,

The eyes that cry, the joints so racked.

Won't ever run again.

The weary legs, the tired breast

the hands which rocked the babes

The lash-ed back which knew no rest,

The portion of the slave

Don't cry for me, when finally,

Ancestral graves I find,

I fixed my gaze, they called me there,

And now, I'll have what's mine.

Ignominious

Never to remain

Seeking lower than you are;

or that perceived as higher,

Bought with censure, and dominion.

Never she, your equal

With no modicum, respect.

Scorn and wanton exploitation,

Not for power, nor for passion.

Your inheritance is wasted

Sweet innocence, so jaded.

Heritage is spurned,

As with your light, diminished, faded.

The selling of your tortured soul,

Her mercy, and command

When head, instead could cradle,

In the bosom of my love.

Ignominious...

Betrayal

Betrayal

Betrayed

Downtrodden

Redeemed

Redemption

It seemed,

Until, she was gone.

None Came To Forewarn

In tandem. Singularity, none.

Alone... a time of old

Purpose found, one and the same,

Sweet chapter, verse untold.

So captivating, giving pause...

No face, nor real dimension, torn.

If this has (and it has) been fated,

None came here, to me, forewarn.

All for which my heart may feel

Or love reveal, is this...

In grace and passion's story

Nothing hidden; only bliss!

My lover, husband, guardian, friend

Who time and strife can't claim,

Entwined in body, till the end

My shield, your glorious name!

Dragons

For Nicholas Charles Peter Miller

"Your dragons are in my blood,"

He wrote.

The words of my beloved mentor

Speaking, fondly, of his home.

Nick Miller – Prince of Rarity.

With fate, inordinately cruel.

To fade and lose that voice,

His tireless instrument, by selfless choice.

What was it, that he had to learn?

Life lost too soon, no stone unturned

Did hero leave, in trying to fight,

A scourge not understood.

The ones remaining, left to find

Their way through void, without your hand.

Your legacy won't ever leave...

Pray, rest in peace, dear Angel-man.

Fly

Should gold be what you yearn to find,

It's sure to never stay

The wicked, soul-less world

Exacts a heavy price to pay.

Though mine may be to wonder why

In wond'ring, there's no peace.

Looking up towards the sky,

Heart aching for release...

Someone... respond in faith, to say,

It doesn't have to be.

Brutish, short, it is for some,

Not universally.

In hope is where the gift does lie

The promise, frailty, whim.

The right to our survival

Must we sink? Or, do we swim?

Don't search for rhyme, nor reason.

For it never will be found.

The secret, is but to endure,

Else lift feet from the ground.

And fly.

Electric Blue

Furious dancing, neon blue

Electric light bulb, glows above.

Discovery, paving ways to prove,

Now, you must choose the realest you.

Imprisoned by our own perception

Always with something amiss

Never put a finger on it

And take for granted, intervention

Why, the galling mystery

That we not see through other's eyes?

And rarely, quietly, whence we do

Why must we, then, act so surprised?

Music; vital; staunchest ally,

Stopped by nothing, only death.

Then someone deigns to play it for us

Strange kind of soliloquy...

Home

Too far, too much, and much too sweet

To live in this cruel world;

Your squeezing hand, with failing beat,

And bouncing auburn curls.

I long to dwell where comfort lies

And all stop saying that, "It's okay,"

Where may my anguish meet demise,

And every one of my babies stay?

A brief encounter, deepest imprint.

Permanent; indelible.

No force on Earth could wrench you from me.

Heaven held the power, still.

I would have faced my torture, over

And again, to spare your space

Am I so worthless, mangled, putrid,

I am denied to see your face?

Will love not cleanse, and bind our treasure,

Bloodlines free, to march, to grow?

Or is all hope but dying ember,

And 'ere we reap, we never sowed?

You mattered.

You were mine.

How I want you to come home.

To Taste Her

Fevered, wild and trembling,

Hearing of his heart's own beat,

Inside his ears.

Intoxicating.

His chest just may be torn apart.

Palms, perspiration,

Labored breath.

Exhilarating!

The smell of her;

The way she moves

Binds every cell, and captivates,

Tormented, in each torrid dream.

Gently undulating hips

With rhythm, she infects him.

The way he moves, is fiercely free

No conscious wish, affecting.

He fights; he fights her power, and still,

In every pore knows...

Resistance to this primal urge,

Oblivion, there goes.

And he will have her.

Don't Look Back

She read the lines, in disbelief

"How could he? Not to me!"

The emptiness engulfed her.

No. He swore he'd never leave.

"I don't know how to be alone.

I don't have time to grieve."

She cried, her hand upon her belly

Brushed by blood-stained, dangling sleeve.

Chasm deep as it is wide,

Appears, and rends asunder

A heart once full of hope and pride,

Must fight, not to go under.

If all you give can count for nought,

What is there to envisage?

Save torment, fear, and thoughts remote

Of dearth in soul, and nothing whole.

A vessel filled with tiny life

Abandoned, and alone.

She won't be first to trod the path.

To build from remnants; dust; a home.

Inconstant, fickle, false, and lost.

How will she dissipate the rage?

Fetish, near-death, twisted lust

She once thought was her final cage.

"Don't you feel free?"she asked herself.

Run, little girl.

Don't ever look back.

Reticence

My reticence should have screamed, not whispered.

As our love-making scorched both sky, and ground,

It howled.

The fates and fortunes, they favour the brave.

But, hasn't it always been thus?

So, how's it, only now, I learn?

Leaves, like tender teardrops, fall in swirls.

No longer useful to adorn,

To slow decay, and start anew.

Still starkly precious, in their aged form

Though comes a heavy cost to pay.

No thing is ever truly lost...

Woods

In dark woods of my thoughts, do dwell
Tall creatures; wild, uncouth, unwell;
Too blighted from their heavenly scorn
To sense, or honour, place to mourn.

They hold within firm, formed dictate
So certain of immobile fate,
They can't taste free, they're rooted still,
No torment in them safe to quell.

And in those woods, no paths emerge
To power past the ancient scourge
A speck of light, I train my eye
Within yearning, search, until I die...

Nothing Gold

If nothing now is gold,

Which colours may then serve,

To heighten sense of victory?

My dreams don't fly as high;

Not high, as they once did.

My wings clipped so, by savagery.

Though I, till now, am not undone.

And never will I be.

For 'tis not my Father's wish, for me.

ABOUT THE AUTHOR

Robyn Kusnetsova (Smith), is a forty six year old, former Special Needs Tutor of Jamaican, and English, extraction. Currently living in Oxford, England, and mother of two adult children, this book marks the final realization of a life-long dream; though she never imagined the experiences that would one day lead to the creation of something, more visceral than she thought herself capable of.

It is her hope that these poems, and pieces of writing, will touch her readers enough to inspire them to enjoy more poetry… or, even begin to write it, for themselves. To break the readers' hearts into a thousand, tiny pieces, and put them back together again; imbued with clarity, and empathy.

Made in the USA
Columbia, SC
15 February 2018